SandCastle 1

What Shape Is It?

Triangles

Mary Elizabeth Salzmann

ABDO
Publishing Company

Published by SandCastle™, an imprint of ABDO Publishing Company, 4940 Viking Drive, Edina, Minnesota 55435.

Printed in the United States.

Cover and Interior Photo credits: Comstock, Corel, PhotoDisc

Library of Congress Cataloging-in-Publication Data

Salzmann, Mary Elizabeth, 1968-
    Triangles / Mary Elizabeth Salzmann.
       p. cm. -- (What shape is it?)
    Summary: Simple text and pictures of common, everyday objects introduce the shape of the triangle.
       ISBN 1-57765-165-0 (alk. paper) -- ISBN 1-57765-280-0 (set)
          1. Triangle--Juvenile literature. [1. Triangle.] I. Title.

QA482 .S354 2000
516'.15--dc21

99-046494

The SandCastle concept, content, and reading method have been reviewed and approved by a national advisory board including literacy specialists, librarians, elementary school teachers, early childhood education professionals, and parents.

Let Us Know

After reading the book, SandCastle would like you to tell us your stories about reading. What is your favorite page? Was there something hard that you needed help with? Share the ups and downs of learning to read. We want to hear from you! To get posted on the Abdo Publishing Company Web site, send us email at:

sandcastle@abdopub.com

About SandCastle™
Nonfiction books for the beginning reader

- Basic concepts of phonics are incorporated with integrated language methods of reading instruction. Most words are short, and phrases, letter sounds, and word sounds are repeated.

- Readability is determined by the number of words in each sentence, the number of characters in each word, and word lists based on curriculum frameworks.

- Full-color photography reinforces word meanings and concepts.

- "Words I Can Read" list at the end of each book teaches basic elements of grammar, helps the reader recognize the words in the text, and builds vocabulary.

- Reading levels are indicated by the number of flags on the castle.

Look for more SandCastle books in these three reading levels:

Level 1 (one flag)	Level 2 (two flags)	Level 3 (three flags)

Grades Pre-K to K 5 or fewer words per page	**Grades K to 1** 5 to 10 words per page	**Grades 1 to 2** 10 to 15 words per page

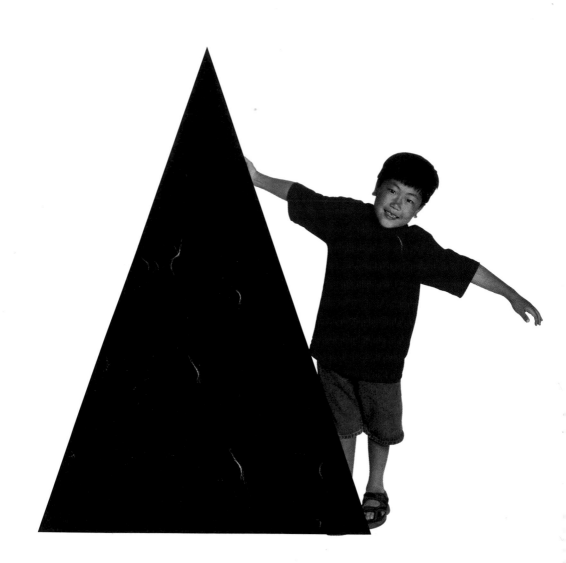

This shape is
a triangle.

5

A triangle has three sides.

7

Some triangles are wide.

This triangle tastes good.

11

This triangle
is wood.

Some triangles
are tall.

15

These triangles
hold us all.

This triangle might fall.

19

Can you find
the triangle?

Words I Can Read

Nouns

A **noun** is a person, place, or thing

shape (SHAYP) p. 5

sides (SYDZ) p. 7

triangle (TRYE-ang-guhl)
pp. 5, 7, 11, 13, 19, 21

triangles (TRYE-ang-guhlz)
pp. 9, 15, 17

wood (WUD) p. 13

Verbs

A **verb** is an action or being word

are (AR) pp. 9, 15

can (KAN) p. 21

fall (FAWL) p. 19

find (FINDE) p. 21

has (HAZ) p. 7

hold (HOHLD) p.17

is (IZ) pp. 5, 13

tastes (TAYSTSS) p. 11

23

▲

Word Families

Words that have the same vowel
and ending letters.

-ide	**-ood**	**-all**
side	good	all
wide	wood	fall
		tall

Find the Triangle

24